A *Good Mistake:*
The *Erik Anderson*
Accident Story

—————⊷ ⟡ ⊶—————

A FATHER'S JOURNAL

ERIK ANDERSON

ISBN 978-1-63874-271-5 (paperback)
ISBN 978-1-63874-272-2 (digital)

Christian Faith Publishing, Inc.
832 Park Avenue
Meadville, PA 16335
www.christianfaithpublishing.com

Printed in the United States of America

INTRODUCTION

When Erik was in the LDS Hospital, his cousin Valerie gave us a new journal so we could record our thoughts and feelings throughout the ordeal. I know I probably should have taken advantage of her wise gesture, but I didn't. Now I am asking everyone involved to write their recollections, hoping that we may publish Erik's story in some form, perhaps through the *Ensign* or anywhere, so that it may be used to inspire others who may be going through a similar trial. I do feel that the memories are still so vivid in my mind that very little detail will be lost. I have relayed this story verbally many times, but it is now time to put it in writing so whoever reads or sees it will know this story is a testimony of the great power of the priesthood, that the Lord does perform miracles in our day, that our Savior does still love us, and that He is Who He says He is. I think I will do this writing in chapters starting with the night of the accident.

THE NIGHT OF
THE ACCIDENT

I was working in unit 8B south at the Victoria House Apartments near Memory Grove, just five minutes away from the LDS Hospital. The manager (Arlynn, I think) came in just before 8:00 p.m. on Tuesday, the twenty-ninth of March 1994 (fourteen years to the day since Erik's baptism by water) and told me that my wife was on the phone for me. I knew immediately that it was bad news. Linda never calls for me at the apartments unless it is an emergency. I was right. It was the kind of news no father ever wants to hear. She said that I needed to go quickly to the LDS Hospital emergency room because Erik had been in an accident. Linda sounded relatively calm, probably because she hadn't been told how severely injured Erik really was. At that instant, I was blessed with a warm assurance that even though very seriously injured, Erik would survive and be okay. I am sure now that even if I had been informed in detail that Erik was hurt far beyond the limits of a fatal injury, I would still have received that strength and comfort from the Lord that I needed to go on. I've always said, and the Lord knows, that I could never be able to handle losing a child like the Furstenaus did when their son (who had just received his mission call) was killed in an auto accident.

I soon arrived at the hospital emergency ward and was told that Erik was already being prepared for surgery (for which they asked and I gave my permission). I was told where to find his friends in a waiting room and that the neurosurgeon would come and talk to me. That meant a head injury! In the waiting room, I found several of Erik's friends, some in tears, others in shock to some degree, and also there were the two Canyon Patrol officers (Salt Lake County deputy sheriffs) who assisted with Erik's rescue. From this group, I was filled in on most of the details of the accident that occurred sometime between 6:30 p.m. and 7:00 p.m. at approximately one mile up from the mouth of Big Cottonwood Canyon. Erik and his friends Brandon, Allen, and Dan Lopez decided to go for a ride up the canyon after work on their Bullet-style motorcycles. Erik's bike was bought new just eleven days prior to the accident. Linda and I were in a quandary whether to help Erik get the bike or not. He was $500 short of the down payment and had asked for our help. We prayed about it, and in spite of Linda's bad feeling about the bike, we decided to help him so he wouldn't lose money on the deal. We knew he would find a way to get another bike anyway. As I reflect on that decision knowing how this all turned out, I feel we were guided, and I haven't any regret. As Erik himself put it, "It was a good mistake."

Erik, Brandon, and Dan invited another friend from work, Buddy Morgan, to ride with them, I believe, on Dan's bike. Erik was usually good about at least taking a helmet and making us think he was wearing it. This time he had taken his helmet, but we were told that he let Buddy wear it because he didn't have one. This gesture of concern for others is very characteristic of bighearted Erik. As they started up the canyon, Erik hit some loose dirt and/or rocks probably along the outer edge of the road. I have wondered why Erik was so close to the edge of the road—whether he was going too fast or maybe they were three abreast or what, I don't know. No one has volunteered the exact circumstances, and I've never pressed for them. I don't really want to know, I guess. I am not blaming and don't want to blame anyone; it doesn't matter because I know that no harm was ever intended. I just hope that no one is feeling any guilt for any reason. Erik has always been daring (we called him our high-risk child), and after four or five previous accidents on motorcycles, he was well aware of the dangers involved. He knew that if he could see an accident about to happen or was losing control, it would best to "lay the bike down" or put it into a skid by applying the brakes. What he apparently wasn't aware of was that Bullet bikes will throw themselves upright when the brakes are applied like that. My theory is that when he hit the brakes, he was propelled upright and off the road, hitting headfirst into the trees and rocks at an estimated seventy-five miles per hour. The impact totaled Erik's new bike (a red, white, and blue Honda CBR600) and was absorbed by the left side of Erik's head and shoulder. He suffered a massive head injury that exposed his brain to the elements, broke his left clavicle, cracked six ribs (two above his heart and four below), collapsed a lung, and gave an assortment of cuts and bruises—easily enough damage to cause instant death. That fact alone tells me that Erik's life was miraculously preserved by Him who has the power to do it, and I thank the Lord daily that Erik is still with us.

Also miraculous was Erik's speedy rescue—as if the stage was set for it before it happened. Instead of Erik's death, his "new life" began. His friends attended to him, and good people immediately stopped to help, one of which went to the nearby 7-Eleven to call for help and found the canyon patrolmen there who then called to the Salt Lake County Fire Department's EMTs for medical assistance. The EMTs found the Life Flight helicopter available practically overhead. They took Erik to the LDS Hospital, where one of the very best neurosurgeons in the country (Robert Peterson) was on duty. There is another part of Erik's rescue that I am attempting to learn more about from the patrolmen, who felt an unseen presence around Erik as he lay there seemingly dead. I'm sure angels were attending to him, perhaps even my mother who passed away just twenty-seven days prior to the accident and maybe my dad who died in 1974. I have on videotape an account of that night as told by our friend (and Erik's former babysitter) Julie Parkin, who was told of Erik's accident by one of the officers who responded to the scene. Julie was not aware that it was Erik the patrolman was talking about until later in his story. She said the officer (I believe his name is Gary Cummins) told her of the "unusual" experience he had as he approached Erik lying still on the ground. Julie describes him as a veteran patrolman who has assisted many such accidents in the canyon over the years and as not a particularly religious person, but he said as he approached Erik, he felt a warm, calm sensation around where Erik lay. He thought he would find a cold, lifeless body but instead was met with this very unusual warmth. Julie said that the patrolmen almost never follow victims to the hospital, but they were compelled to do so with Erik. We (Erik and I) have a strong desire to talk to this patrolman and hear his version of the event, and I'm sure he would be interested to see how Erik is doing today. It hadn't occurred to me at the hospital that it was odd for the patrolmen to be there, but as I think about it now, they were really concerned about Erik. If every policeman followed every accident victim to the hospital, there wouldn't be any left to patrol the streets!

Not long after I arrived at the hospital, Dr. Peterson called me in to talk about the extent of Erik's injuries and show me the x-rays. Dr. Peterson talked very upbeat and businesslike about the injuries without telling me at that time how surprised he was that Erik was still alive and that he really didn't think Erik would survive the surgery or the night at most. I was impressed with Dr. Peterson and felt assured that Erik was in the care of a very skilled and competent doctor. I knew Erik was also in the hands of the Lord and that if it were His will to take Erik, He would have taken him upon impact. Linda arrived at the hospital and joined me with Dr. Peterson just as he was informed that Erik was prepped and ready for the operation. The doctor said the x-rays indicated at least fifteen fractures of Erik's skull and that the surgery would take about two to two and a half hours to complete. I wanted Erik to have a priesthood blessing before the operation but was strongly advised against it. I'm glad we waited because I am sure I wouldn't have wanted see Erik in that condition or lay my hands on his badly shattered head. Instead we went to a small room in the hospital that served as a chapel where we prayed for Erik and all who attended to him. We again were blessed with that peaceful, calm, warm feeling that somehow Erik would beat these enormous odds and recover. Then we waited.

AT THE LDS HOSPITAL

After more than four hours in surgery, Dr. Peterson finally came to us with the news that Erik had made it through. He said it took longer than he thought because the extent of Erik's injuries was far worse than the x-rays had indicated. Erik had more than three fractures on his skull. He also said that he felt as though he had just put Humpty Dumpty back together again. I asked Dr. Peterson to tell us honestly what to expect, what he truly felt would happen with Erik. His answer was remarkable to me and perhaps unprecedented. He said that normally he knew exactly what to tell family members after dealing with a similar head injury, that they should basically expect the worst and start preparing funeral arrangements. "But this time," he said, "I just don't know."

Dr. Peterson came to Utah from his home state of Florida, and I am quite sure he isn't from LDS. I took his response as about the most positive thing that a man in his position could give us. He surely couldn't say that he felt Erik would recover for sure (I doubt he really believed he would), but he did say that Erik's case was different from what he normally sees happen. One of the most common causes of death due to head trauma is the swelling of the brain. Dr. Peterson was surprised to find very little swelling of Erik's brain—so little that he skipped the normal SOP of installing a small shunt in his brain designed for nurses to monitor the degree of swelling. He later did put one in at the insistence of the nurses because they were getting nervous, not believing there wasn't some swelling they should be monitoring!

Dr. Peterson told us that if Erik did recover, the last thing to come back to him would be his speech because the part of his brain that controls speech had sustained the most damage. He said he had pulled bone fragments from that area. He also said to expect some hearing loss in the left ear because of the severe damage to the left side of his head. He called the damage "bilateral," meaning the direct impact came to the side of his head rather than to the front or back. That meant that Erik's face was virtually undamaged. I later realized how remarkable the fact was that his ribs were cracked above and below his heart and the ribs directly over Erik's tender heart were protected. This was just another of the many, many little miracles that combined to make up Erik's totally miraculous recovery.

We were now able to see Erik in the ICU and give him a priesthood blessing. During the surgery, I kept wondering if I would be emotionally able to give Erik the blessing. As his father, I might be tempted to go against Heavenly Father's will and just command Erik to live and return to normal or even "rise up and walk." I knew I had the power to do that, but I did not want to put my personal desire ahead of the Lord's will. My struggle was quickly resolved as I again realized that it was the Lord's will for Erik to live and that I could give this blessing just as I have given many others: simply by the Spirit. I would just be the vocal medium by and through which the Lord would pronounce His blessing for Erik. It has always been the highest honor and privilege I have had to serve directly with the Lord to bless the lives of others, and I was anxious to be able to do it now for my own son. It was a very special time for me, and I felt the Spirit very strongly. I was grateful for the assistance and company of Brandon and his father, Fred Allen, and, of course, the presence of Linda, Natalie, and Damon. (I am sure that other family members and/or friends were present, but I can't remember them all.) Fred anointed Erik, and the words of the sealing blessing came to me easily and with great comfort through the Spirit directly from the Lord. I've never felt closer to the Lord in my life. With our hands resting gently on Erik's reconstructed skull, his head shaved (except for the hair just above his neck), and skin being held together with at least fifty large staples forming an S pattern across the top of his head, winding down the back and left side and ending behind his left ear, he was given an incredible promise of complete and rapid restoration. I'm wondering if the nurses and other attendants who heard the blessing, not being aware of the power of the priesthood, pitied us for actually believing that such promises could ever come true in this case. I had asked Dr. Peterson if he had ever seen a victim of such severe injuries as Erik's survive them. He said that he hadn't and that he had seen much less severe injuries that have proved fatal to the victims. But Erik's blessing promised that he would not have these things that normally occur and often cause death with head injuries and that he would be able to recover and function on his own. He was told that he would be able to work, marry, and raise a family and have his usual sense of humor and tender heart and other equally unlikely-to-happen things.

The will of the Lord had been declared! And as we've been taught in the church, we simply expect all the things promised in that blessing to happen. In Dr. Peterson's professional words, "Erik's hand has been dealt. We can now only wait and see what those cards are." Of course, after hearing the words of Erik's blessing, we knew what those "cards" were. Erik's "hand" was a winning blessing from the Lord that would defy and beat all earthly odds. Erik had always seemed to be able to beat the odds, but this time, beating these odds was clearly a gift from God.

Erik's blessing also said his recovery would be speedy or quicker than normal. Since a normal recovery of this nature takes ten years or more, we knew that this did not mean Erik would be home in a week or two and back to work in a month. We realized that *speedy* in this case could mean five years of recovery and therapy before Erik was back to work and able to function on his own. Exactly how long the recovery would be, we weren't sure. We were only sure that there would be a recovery that wouldn't take as long as normal. So we scheduled our lives to include as much time daily as possible to be with Erik. Fortunately for me, I was blessed with employers (DuMayne Gilson and John West at Utah Railway Company) who were compassionately and genuinely interested in Erik and allowed me to take whatever time off I needed to be with Erik without being docked any pay. I will always be grateful to them for their caring attitude. I will always be grateful also to the hundreds of friends and family members who came to the hospital, called, or wrote to express their concern and add their faith and prayers to ours. Erik's name was on many different temples' prayer rolls and was even prayed for by ministers of other religions.

Throughout Erik's nearly three months in three hospitals, there wasn't a single day he didn't have visitors. I was truly amazed at the number of people who responded to Erik's and our needs. I hadn't realized how many friends Erik really had, especially girlfriends! While Erik was in the ICU at the LDS Hospital, there was rarely an empty chair in the waiting room. Many, many people came to see Erik and also to be with and comfort us (the immediate family). We were already so comforted by the Comforter Himself that we ended up passing on our comfort to many of those who came to comfort us. This happened so often that Linda and I began to wonder if there was something wrong with us because we weren't as distraught as we should have been!

The answer to that question came to us on Saturday, April 2, 1994, just four days after the accident. It came to us through an apostle of the Lord, Richard G. Scott, who prepared and delivered a general conference address that I swear was written just for us. The title of his talk was "To Be Healed" in which he quoted Mosiah 24:13–15 and explained how the Lord visits His people in their afflictions, makes their burdens light, and strengthens those who covenant with Him and submit to His will. Elder Scott talked specifically about how this applies to us today and to those who are sick or injured. He testified (and we found this to be true) that "love is a potent healer." I hope someday Elder Scott will read this account of Erik's story and will know how important his message was to us and how much we appreciate him.

Elder Scott also pointed out in verse 14 of Mosiah 24 that the Lord, in return for easing our burdens, asked us to "stand as witnesses for me hereafter." This I have done many times and will gladly continue to do for the rest of my life. The Lord does indeed visit His people in their afflictions and does continue to perform miracles through His servants and His priesthood. In the same conference, Elder Malcolm Jepson gave an address that was of a similar theme (titled "A Divine Prescription for Spiritual Healing") in which we found additional comfort. He talked about spiritual healing, but what I remember most was when Elder Jepson "confessed" that as a medical doctor, he has never actually healed anyone. All he ever did, he said, was to provide the environment in which his patients could be healed by the power and will of the Lord. It reminded me of Dr. Peterson, who said that all he did was put Erik's head back together and then wait and see what cards he had been dealt. Elder Jepson's talk also gave us hope that Erik would not only be healed physically but that this experience would be beneficial in the healing of his ailing spirit.

While Erik lay in the ICU still in a deep coma, it seemed that the nurses were always prepared for and totally expecting Erik to experience any or all of the normal and often fatal aftereffects of severe head trauma. One of his many monitors measured his body temperature and showed that it was erratic; this was because the part of his brain that controls it was damaged. They monitored the swelling in his brain and never found a serious problem. They monitored his blood pressure and became alarmed when it indicated that he might be bleeding internally. They gave him some new blood one time, and there was no further problem. Erik never even experienced seizures that almost always occur with head injuries. Throughout his intensive care, his vital signs fluctuated only within normal ranges, and all those attending to Erik's recovery seemed surprised, if not amazed, with his progress. Since Erik had not yet opened his eyes, we were a little surprised when they told us that after one week in the ICU, he was going to be moved to a semiprivate room and would begin receiving some physical therapy.

Linda and I had planned to celebrate our twenty-fifth wedding anniversary by taking the kids with us to Las Vegas, but instead we spent our anniversary (April 1) in the hospital. I remember that as my birthday (April 11) approached, I kept telling Erik that all I wanted from him for my birthday was to be able to see his blue eyes again. We were encouraged by the nurses to try stimulating Erik by talking to him. I was delighted when Erik did manage to partially fulfill my request by getting one eye (his left, I believe) to open partway on my birthday. Also, when I came to visit, his room was decorated with a banner wishing me a happy birthday, and it was signed by everyone who was there—including Erik! I believe that Natalie, Gavin, and/or Damon helped Erik sign his name. It was a wonderful surprise and a memorable birthday.

We were told that Erik would not be staying for very long in that room or even in the LDS Hospital. The plan was for him to be transferred to an intermediate care facility where he would be receiving more preliminary therapy and healing time until he would be evaluated as ready to begin more rigorous therapy at the University of Utah medical center. Comas are rated by stages, and Erik had to advance to a certain stage of awareness to receive occupational and speech therapy. We chose to take him to the Doxey-Hatch Medical Center on Thirty-Ninth South and Thirteenth East, much closer to home and work. We were told to expect Erik to remain at Doxey-Hatch for three (or possibly more) months, but I felt at the time that Erik's speedy recovery would get him to the U of U sooner than that. We had virtually nonstop visitors and calls while Erik was at the LDS Hospital, but one visit that perhaps touched me most was from Bob and Janette Furstenau, who knew exactly what we were going through emotionally and spiritually. It really meant a lot to have them visit us. I remember telling Bishop Bob that when his son died, I couldn't understand how they seemed to be able to handle the loss better than I did. But now, by experiencing the Lord's love and having Him carry my burden, I understood.

AT DOXEY-HATCH

My earliest recollection of Erik's stay at Doxey-Hatch (DH) was our concern that his insurance may not cover the projected length of his time there. We were very thankful that Erik was working full-time and qualified for insurance coverage. He had chosen FHP, and despite their reputation with some doctors and others we talked to (who said FHP was okay until you needed them), we had relatively little problem dealing with them. But as I recall, our concern was that FHP would only approve a one-month coverage to begin with, and Erik was considered to be at least three months away from being ready for rehab at the U of U. "Not to worry," as the saying goes. Erik's speedy recovery had him ready to leave DH after only two weeks!

During this brief stay, I recall many incidents and memories. I continued to be amazed at the many visitors Erik received and the many cards, flowers, balloons, stuffed animals, and other offerings of affection given to him. All these things served to stimulate Erik, awaken his emotions, and get him to respond. Among the items given to him was a Utah Jazz hat from Rob Duehlmeier, his work supervisor, and a cassette tape of one of Erik's favorite groups, the Steve Miller Band, from Linda's boss, Carol Barrett. He also had some foam rubber balls, and I would try to get him to "throw" them to me. His eyes were open now, and he appeared to be awake but was still in a coma. Erik tells us now that he remembers nothing at all of being at the LDS Hospital or at DH. But he would, at times, respond a little to our repeated attempts to stimulate him. He would grasp the foam ball, and as his elbow rested beside him on the bed, he would let his arm fall as he released the ball. All these little things meant so much to us because they showed progress in his recovery.

Erik had literally lost all ability to do anything for himself and was like an infant trying to learn everything for the first time.

Erik became an instant favorite of the staff at DH because he was making such an amazing and unprecedented recovery from such a serious injury. We kept looking for the little signs of progress and found them almost daily. Sometimes we would see big steps. The physical therapists worked on his legs and arms and soon had him vertical for the first time since the accident. They would help him up on his feet and, with one man under each arm, "walk" him down the hall by getting him to drag one foot forward at a time. Erik wasn't allowed to eat or drink because of the possibility he would choke, so his mouth was always dry. I realized that a dry mouth was a good stimulator when one day, as the therapists were walking Erik down a hall, they passed a drinking fountain and he tried desperately to turn to the fountain for a drink. He became very irritated when they wouldn't let him do it. We were delighted to see him try!

We were warned that Erik, as a result of his head injury, would no doubt have mood swings and often become irritated. At this point, we were always glad to see him show any kind of emotion, even irritation. And we saw plenty of irritation in the weeks to follow! We were encouraged to even try stirring Erik's emotions by bringing in the family pet. So when we brought in Rocky, our small but grumpy dog, to visit Erik, both became a little irritated! Erik had always teased Rocky until he growled, and although Rocky really handled the confusion of a crowded room surprisingly well, Erik pushed him away. And Rocky growled.

I videotaped that moment and some other time that I visited, and I am glad I did. I wasn't sure that I should or wanted to put Erik on videotape in that condition, but I felt prompted to do it anyway. That tape has since proven valuable in helping Erik realize how much improvement he has made since that time. One day after he had been home for several months, he was frustrated and probably thought he wasn't going to get any better and wouldn't ever be able to get married and have a home and family like his friends were doing. He told me that he didn't like his "new life." I knew at that instant why I had videotaped him at DH. I said, "Erik, I want you to see something." After viewing the tape and with tears in his eyes, he realized how blessed he was to be able to do all that he was able to do at the time. The tape has also been used at Linda's school for health classes (Linda and Erik have been there to show it) and was even used by our neighbor, Paul Reynolds, for one of his school assignments.

It's probably for the best that Erik doesn't remember all the DH experiences because some of them involved some loss of dignity and may have been embarrassing for him. The nurses and aides along with the occupational therapists had to help Erik shower and get dressed for the first time since his accident. But Erik was still most remembered at DH for the amazingly fast recovery of his strength and the many ways he expressed his irritation. I discovered how much hand strength he had recovered when one day he got hold of me by my throat and wouldn't let go! He also demonstrated his grasp to Natalie by grabbing and holding on to her hair. And he wore his uncle Dusty down more than once. My brother was willing and able to spend a lot of time with Erik and left his family in Burley, Idaho, to stay day and night with him. Erik needed around-the-clock supervision primarily to keep him from his favorite expression of irritation: pulling out of his body all of the tubes that were there to keep him alive. He was hooked up to a respirator by a tube surgically implanted through his neck and throat and was being fed by a tube to his stomach that went through his nose. I can understand his irritation; one doesn't need a head trauma to hate the discomfort of tubes like that. Erik soon learned that he could grab those tubes and pull them out to relieve his discomfort. And he did it dozens of times despite the close watch of all his attendants.

Our ward (Union 16) members graciously accepted assignments to sit with Erik, with their main charge being to keep him from pulling his tubes out. Many thought they would just bring reading material and other activities to keep themselves awake and pass the time. Almost all reported that they spent all their time actively engaged with Erik in a spirited game of wits. Erik learned to slyly lay his hand on his pillow around the top of his head as if he were just resting. Then the moment his attendants diverted their attention, even if just brief enough to look at the clock, he would bring his arm down and rid himself of all those tubes in a second. Actually, I think this "game" was good therapy for him, and he was still officially in a coma! But he didn't understand that he needed the tubes in him to stay alive, so he became a little irritated at the DH staff every time they had to reinsert the tubes.

Erik had become so proficient at removing his tubes that the staff at DH decided to take more drastic measures to prevent him from succeeding at this game. Normally, all it took to keep someone from pulling their tubes out was to put large "mittens" on their hands. These mittens resembled boxing gloves put on backward, so the palms of the hands were heavily padded to prevent the wearer from gripping anything. But Erik (still in a coma) figured out that he could turn the mittens around so the padding was on the back of his hand, allowing him to grip the tubes. The next step in this ongoing game was for the staff to tie the mittens and Erik's hands securely to the side rails of his bed. That should do it! Nope. Erik's response was to somehow contort his body to lean far enough to the side, take his tubes to his hands, turn his mittens, and yank. I was told that one time he actually broke the cloth ties holding the mittens to the rail.

Erik also felt that he should be able to get out of bed on his own for whatever reason he wanted. We got a real scare when we were informed that Erik had managed get out of his restraints and make his way off the end of his bed. Since his leg strength was still not sufficient to hold his body weight (even though he had lost forty pounds since the accident), he fell to the floor and hit his fragile head on the foot of the bed. Fortunately, no more damage was done to his skull (how could there be?), but he did need stitches to close a small gash between his eyebrows. The DH staff responded by tying Erik's arms and legs to the bed rails and adding bedsheets rolled and tied to the rails, crisscrossing Erik's chest! "Let's see you get out of this, Erik!" they said. Erik had been given the nickname of Humpty Dumpty at the LDS Hospital, and now at DH, he earned a new one: Houdini! And yes, he did still manage to free himself from those restraints somehow. All we could do was have someone there watching Erik every minute of every day and arm wrestle with him as he continued trying to rid himself of his discomforts and trying to get up to go somewhere. Many of us will testify how much and how quickly his strength was returning to him, especially Uncle Dusty and Allen Howard.

Erik was always a strong, agile, quick, and wiry athlete. Though not big (five feet and nine inches, 170 pounds), he was tough enough for high school football. He was a hot-dog skier and excelled in baseball, the kind of outfielder that would climb a fence to rob a batter's home run. He was the only eleven-year-old little leaguer who I've ever seen make a diving, horizontal catch of a line drive to left field. Ever since Erik was very young and would go with me to my Union Pacific softball games at White Park, I had always wanted to be able to play county recreational softball with my son or sons. I fulfilled that dream by playing with Erik (and later, his brother Damon) on a team called "Norrells" that was organized by another father-son duo, Rick and Rick Jr. Norris and Brian Sorrell, all longtime friends. After Erik's accident put him out for the season (at least), I didn't know whether I wanted to play without him or not. When Rick Jr. called and asked for Erik's jersey, I thought it was so he could give it to whoever replaced Erik on the team. But when Rick said he wanted to hang Erik's jersey (with the number 1) in the dugout during every game and dedicate the season to him, I knew that I wanted to play with them knowing that Erik would at least be there in spirit. I got off to a good start and enjoyed playing well under the inspiration of Erik's jersey for two games. My season also came to an early end on April 23 or 24 when, in the last inning of the game played on the asphalt-like infield of Harmony Park, I broke my right ankle (tibia) while making a bad hook slide into second base (I did manage to score, and we won the game). I remember limping into DH after the game, knowing my foot was broken but wanting to see Erik and having Linda and Bishop Rich Jensen insist that I go across the street to the St. Mark's Hospital for x-rays. I was in a cast and on crutches for about a month and in a walking cast for about two more months. I received a lot of sympathy from the DH staff but also a lot of razzing and advice that I was getting brittle in my advancing age (forty-eight) and should have sense enough to quit playing kid games. But deep in my heart, I felt (or at least strongly desired) that both Erik and I would be back out on the softball field and playing together again. But for the time being, we just focused on our recoveries.

Natalie and Damon were very loyal in visiting and "stimulating" Erik as often as possible. Fun-loving Damon would entertain the staff and visitors to the point that we thought he might be invited to leave, but his antics were tolerated and even appreciated by some who needed a little levity in their lives. One of his favorite pastimes would be to put on a helmet (borrowed from one of Erik's motorcycle-riding visitors) and do wheelies in a wheelchair out in the hallway. Erik's room was on the second floor of the northeast wing at DH, which had many empty rooms. That was good because there was often a lot of noisy laughter and confusion coming from Erik's room. The activity was good and bad for Erik; it was stimulating but also exhausting and increased his irritation.

We were always grateful that so many people came to visit. We were also a little concerned about some of the unfamiliar (to us) young ladies who would spend a lot of time with Erik, talking to him and stroking him like they had been intimate friends. We began to wonder what their expectations were if and when Erik recovered. But in any event, we were glad that we weren't left with the full-time effort of being the only ones to tend to Erik during this important time of extra need. Being close to the home of Grandpa and Grandma Seddon and Maureen was a great blessing also, allowing Grandpa to walk to DH to visit Erik, which he did often. I don't think Erik was ever without someone there or nearby.

I am now trying to get as many people as possible who were involved with Erik and us to write or tell on video what they remember most about this experience. I'm sure there are some incidents that I've forgotten about or haven't heard yet. Erik made so much progress in the two weeks he spent at DH that he was then considered ready to move on to the University of Utah rehab facility for more intensive and diverse therapy. Although it meant a longer drive for us to be with Erik each day, we were ready.

AT THE UNIVERSITY OF UTAH REHABILITATION CENTER

I remember the ride from DH to the U of U quite clearly. It was the first time I noticed that Erik seemed interested in what was going on around him. He seemed more alert and less agitated. He was sitting up in a wheelchair in the back of a van. I was invited to ride with him, and sporting a Utah Jazz purple cast on my right foot, I struggled with my crutches to get into the front seat of the van. I looked back and watched Erik closely during the ride, and I felt that he was really making progress as he sat leaning forward with his elbows on the arms of the wheelchair, looking first out one window then out another. His expression was still distant but much improved from two weeks earlier when he was transported to DH from the LDS hospital in an ambulance. The van driver was amazed at Erik's condition, considering the severity of his injuries. When we arrived at the U of U admitting entrance, one of the aides assisting us asked me if Erik and I had been in the same accident. It was a logical and reasonable question, but it made me laugh. I told him, "No, I was dumb enough to find one of my own."

Erik tells us now that he has no recollection of the ride to the U of U even though it appeared to me that he was aware of what was going on around him. He says that his first awareness came about a month after he arrived at the U of U and that he remembers nothing of the accident, the bike ride, or being at the LDS hospital or DH. His last memory was of going to work the day of the accident. It must have been hard for him to come around and wonder if he was in some horrible nightmare or something. He still couldn't speak and couldn't ask where he was or what happened to him. And we couldn't tell if he was aware enough to understand. But we were in the habit of telling him details about his situation each day as a form of stimulation, so I think he soon realized that he had been in a terrible accident. He tells me now that one of his earliest recollections of coming to is finding himself in the shower with a female aide and thinking, *What's going on?!*

Erik was put in a room with a young man named Britton(?) from Bountiful who suffered a serious head injury in an automobile accident. He was also making a good recovery but was experiencing more agitation than Erik. One day, we came to see Erik, and he wasn't in his room. The nurses said they had to move Erik to another room because his roommate apparently didn't want Erik in his room and threatened some kind of harm. I was glad the nurses were aware of potential problems and were taking measures to protect their patients.

Even though Erik's room was hard to find and deep in the rehab center at the U of U, he still had a continual flow of visitors, including girls he had met and/or dated. There were three particularly loyal young ladies, Angie, Kim (and her mother), and Dana, who came almost as often as we did. I think they were a good stimulation for Erik, but we wondered just how good when we came into Erik's room one day and found Dana lying in bed with him. I'm sure it was done in innocence, but that was going the extra mile!

Erik did continue to make progress as he was being given physical, speech, occupational, and family/friend therapy. We saw a lot of little things that were encouraging and some big things that really made us see he would recover. For several weeks, he still couldn't or wouldn't eat or drink, so he still had the tubes in him. Yes, he still pulled them out every chance he could. We encouraged him to drink as much as possible and to just eat a bite or two. The doctors were less and less worried about him aspirating and more concerned about him being able to eat enough to be able to get rid of those darned tubes and also nourish his body. He took a liking to apricot nectar and would also drink apple juice and grape juice. He began to drink more and more, but a problem came of this. If the aides weren't able to come often enough to take Erik to the bathroom, he would take it upon himself to roll to the edge of the bed and relieve himself on the floor! It only took a couple times of cleaning up before the aides checked on him more often.

The first intelligible word I heard Erik speak came as I entered his room one day, riding my crutches. He looked at me and said, "Crutches," as I leaned them against the wall. It was a great thrill for me to hear him say that one word and see him put on that one-sided grin of his. The first time I heard him laugh out loud was also a great moment of excitement and hope. On one visit, as we looked for ways to pass time that might stimulate Erik, I took a rubber surgical glove and, imitating an episode of *M*A*S*H** where Hawkeye and BJ (or maybe Trapper) were playing a form of volleyball with an inflated glove, I blew the glove full of air and tied it at the wrist. As we batted the glove around the room and above Erik, he laughed out loud and soon tried hitting the glove with his hand. I've never had such an exhilarating time!

This became a regular activity with each visit, and I'll always remember the day Erik decided he wanted to blow up the glove and tie it himself. He was able to blow air into it but struggled trying to tie it. I decided to not do it for him and wondered how soon he would give up in a fit of frustration. I swear it was fifteen minutes that he worked on that project, and I was again thrilled at his effort and amazed that he wasn't showing agitation. He finally found a way to solve his problem by removing some of the air in the glove; that gave him more of the wrist to tie. He was proud of himself, and so was I. We were told that people with serious head trauma would have trouble solving problems and may be able to relearn things they already knew but would have difficulty learning new things. This little event demonstrated to me that Erik would indeed be an exception to these norms. His priesthood blessing promised that he would, and I could see it happening. Erik had learned something new and had solved a problem.

Erik laughed more and more often each time we visited as we played glove volleyball, and Damon entertained us all by stunt-walking on my crutches. I think it was Natalie and Gavin who tried playing simple card games with Erik. He responded by relearning and getting hooked on "War." He brought out the playing cards to play War with just about everyone who visited. Erik also enjoyed getting out of his room for a wheelchair ride all over the hospital. We often visited the cafeteria for some frozen yogurt. The more we could get Erik to eat, the sooner he could get rid of the feeding tube. No matter how long our strolls were, Erik would express his desire to stay out of his room by putting his hands on the doorjamb to block our entrance.

Erik had many very good nurses (one of our favorites was named Jeff), aides, and therapists who took a genuine interest in and worked well with him. I remember sitting in with Charlie Krueger, the speech therapist, as he would work with Erik by showing him flash cards with pictures, trying to get him to say the word that described them. Erik would be rewarded with a chocolate shake if he responded. Charlie was always positive, optimistic, and encouraging as he worked with Erik but later admitted to wondering if Erik would ever be able to converse to any large degree. He explained that Erik would be able to comprehend something he saw better than something he heard, which was normal for head injury victims. I don't know if Clint Cressall simply understood that or was inspired to give Erik a writing board with dry markers so we could write messages to him. Erik did respond well to written communication by pointing to multiple-choice answers to our questions. We could see progress with this form of communication and prayed for his eventual ability to verbalize and comprehend audible conversation.

Erik's favorite therapist was Ann Summers who patiently gave him daily physical therapy. She still remembers Erik fondly today (over four years later) as always being "ready to go," willing, and cooperative. With Ann's work, Erik soon began to gain strength and walk on his own. His pace was unsteady and slow, but he had learned to walk again. Grandpa Seddon spent many days with Erik in therapy and said he seemed to really enjoy doing exercises in the swimming pool. We continued to do as many stimulating activities as we could during our daily visits, which included shooting baskets on the patio court just outside Erik's room. Erik would sit in his wheelchair out by the court and look as if he wanted to be playing with us (he still wasn't able to speak in sentences). When we gave him the ball, he would attempt a shot at the hoop, mustering what strength he had. We would quit playing once he became agitated when he couldn't hit the rim. We all enjoyed the various activities sponsored by the occupational therapists such as the outdoor barbecues and the weekly dinners. My personal favorite activity was being invited to accompany Erik and a small group of other patients to a Buzz baseball game at Franklin Quest. I can't remember who we played or who won the game, but I do remember Erik's choice of headwear. His friend, Danny Creer, had given Erik a ball cap that had a built-in blond ponytail. Danny knew Erik would be upset when he became aware the doctors had to remove all his hair, so he gave him the false locks to wear until he could regrow his real ones. Actually, the doctors only removed the hair off the top of Erik's head, so he had shoulder-length hair extending from behind one ear, around the back of his head, and to the other ear. He looked like a clown, so we asked the aides to complete the hair removal. Linda and I hoped Erik would decide that he liked his hair short because it was easier to maintain, made him look older (more mature), and because we liked short hair better. But Erik thought the hat with the blonde ponytail looked good, and maybe that gave him a sense of confidence because he started flirting with about every girl he saw at the ballpark!

I felt very encouraged seeing Erik get out in public again but wondered how he would react when we took him back to the hospital and left him there again. Once, when we were walking outside of the hospital, I had wondered about taking Erik for a little ride around the parking lots in the truck. I got permission from the nurse to do it, and Erik really seemed to enjoy the ride. But when I tried to take him back, he didn't want to get out of the truck. I was finally able to get him out but only after lengthy persuasion. Fortunately, I didn't have any trouble getting him to return after the ballgame, probably because of the cute female therapist who he willingly followed inside! But ever since the first time I took Erik for a short ride, he wanted to get in the car or truck and go somewhere just about every time we visited. Our rides gradually extended further from the hospital, and I found myself looking forward to the time we could take Erik home for good.

We soon learned that if we were going on an extended walk or ride, we had to make sure Erik visited the restroom before we went because one time, as we were outside walking back toward the main hospital entrance, Erik turned off the sidewalk and onto the lawn near the helicopter pad. We thought that maybe he wanted to sit on the grass and rest awhile. Instead Erik felt the need to relieve himself, and because he still hadn't relearned it wasn't appropriate behavior to do it on the front lawn of the hospital, he proceeded. Linda and I decided that any effort to stop him would only cause greater problems, so we just tried to stand in front of him in a useless attempt for some degree of modesty. The couple who was walking toward us on the sidewalk suddenly changed their course to the other side of the road! We were warned that head trauma caused the victims to lose their recognition of what was appropriate behavior, and we saw what they meant!

As Erik grew stronger and was eating more and more, he was finally permanently relieved of the feeding tubes in his nose. Around the first part of June, we were told that he would be allowed to make a weekend home visit mainly to see how many problems he would encounter while living at home. Since his bedroom was in the basement, his therapists guessed that he would at least have trouble going up and/or down the stairs. I feared that once at home, he would not want to return to the hospital. He was still not able to speak in complete sentences, but he made it clear that he was ready to go home. When we got home, he went in the back door and immediately went downstairs to his room on his own, no problem. I wasn't even aware that he had gone down; it happened so fast. The weekend went well, and several times I explained that we would be taking him back to the hospital and leaving him there again, hoping he wouldn't get mad when we did. We were relieved when he returned willingly without getting upset. The visit went so well that no further trial runs were necessary. Erik was released on June 17 to come home for good.

HOME AGAIN

Today is Erik's twenty-eighth birthday. I told him that I used to be amazed he had made it through another year, to see another birthday. It has now been almost six years since the accident. I am no longer amazed that he lived to be another year older. I believe he will live to become a grandfather like I am now for the second time in the last fourteen months. Erik's wife, Sam (Sandra), just gave birth to Khristian, their second son, to be a pal to their firstborn son, Levi. There was a time just after the accident when very few of us thought the day would come when Erik would be back to work, be ordained an Elder, be married, and be a father living in a new home.

When Erik came home to stay, the only medication he was on was to help his knee resist the buildup of calcium that caused stiffness. Besides the stiff knee that hindered his ability to run, he still suffered from double vision and struggled to find the words he needed to express himself in complete sentences. He still received a lot of physical and speech therapy. We also had to continue to remind Erik what was considered appropriate behavior and what was not. It was, in some ways, as if Erik was thrust back in time and we were being given the opportunity to raise him from childhood a second time. This time around was different because we had help from Natalie and Damon. Damon made the comment that he felt he had traded places with Erik and had become the big brother. I think he liked being the little brother better, but he has done well to adjust and help Erik in any way he can.

Natalie had been taking American Sign Language classes at the U of U, and one evening, when we were waiting for our dinner to be served at Italian Village, it occurred to her to teach Erik some signs to see if it would help him to communicate better. Erik caught on quickly, and making signs seemed to help him remember the words he wanted to say. We were delighted with this new development and encouraged by still more evidence that Erik was able to learn new things. I was determined to learn sign language also, thinking that maybe it was going to be the best way to communicate with Erik in the future. But as Erik learned new signs, his verbal skills began to return. And I never learned sign language.

We were happy to have Erik at home again, and we looked for new ways to assist with his ongoing therapy and recovery. He continued to receive speech therapy at the U of U, and to give him the chance to regain muscle tone, weight, and physical strength, we purchased a family membership to the Sports Mall. Erik was eager to go and work out, especially when he met some of the cute female trainers. We also enjoyed playing racquetball but had to be careful to see that Erik was not hit in the head with the ball or a racket. That was not really a problem at first as Erik was only able to stand in one spot and, with one hand in his pocket, weakly swing at the ball only if it came near where he was standing. Many times he would miss hitting the ball, and I would ask him how many balls he saw coming toward him. He would grin, shut one eye, and hold up three or four fingers. I thought again of when we were advised that Erik would likely become easily frustrated, upset, moody, etc., but this activity on the racquetball courts indicated to me that he was able to handle himself calmly and with patience. He was only a little more discouraged when he went skiing and soon found that he was not going to regain his hot-dog, fast-down-the-hill style again and that from then on, he had to wear a helmet and take it easy.

Soon after Erik's release from the hospital, he and I decided to watch our softball team, the Sharks, at Harmony Park. With Erik sporting an eye patch to help his double vision and I with my right foot in a walking cast, we approached the dugout. The warm, emotional reception Erik received from our teammates brought a tear to my eye. Erik's jersey was still hanging on the dugout fence. I don't remember who won the game, but I will always remember the still-crooked smile that brightened Erik's face. We accepted the fact that we were out for the summer and fall seasons, but we looked forward to the spring when we felt determined to rejoin the team in practice.

Erik progressed well with his physical redevelopment at the Sports Mall, and by springtime he was running the racquetball court quite well and gave me a sweaty workout each time we played. He was strong and in good shape having regained the forty-plus pounds he lost in the hospitals, but he was still hampered by stiffness in his knee. As planned, we were able to rejoin our softball team in the spring. When the coach put Erik in the outfield at the first practice, he still had trouble deciding which of the two or three balls he saw coming at him to catch. His verbal skills were improving but were still a struggle for him. But I was impressed by his confidence in himself, and he did show some frustration when the coach wouldn't let him play as long or at the position he wanted. Coach Norris was simply trying to protect Erik. He didn't want to risk Erik getting a hit in the head with the ball or a bat or a fist that would cause a fatal injury. I'm glad he was concerned about Erik as much as I was, but I still had mixed emotions. I was afraid of Erik getting hurt too, but I also wanted him to have the chance to gain more confidence and prove to himself that he could play. Erik knew he wasn't the agile, wiry athlete he once was, but he at least wanted to play part of the time. If he didn't get into the game at all, he would get angry.

The coach's worry was justified in one competitive, hard-fought game at Sandy Park. I wasn't at the game and am not real certain of the details of this incident, but as I understand it, Erik was playing catcher when an opposing player tried to score and Erik blocked the plate. The runner took exception and took a swing at Erik's head. Erik was able to duck enough to only receive a glancing blow from the runner's elbow that opened a cut above his eye. Everyone on our team was protective of Erik, and our bench quickly cleared as they ran to his defense. The runner surely regretted taking a cheap shot at Erik when big Dave Anderson (no relation), our first baseman, returned the blow. This episode failed to dampen Erik's desire to play but increased my worry when he did play.

During the time Erik was off work, he kept in touch with many people at DOD (Harmon Music Group). I think his supervisors wanted to see him recover enough to be able to return to his former job but were wary of letting him come back too soon. I'm sure that they were afraid he wouldn't be able to do the work and that if they couldn't find something he could do, they would have to terminate him, which would put an end to his medical benefits. In an effort to help Erik return to his job, they gave him some tools and an old board or two to practice on at home. I feel that this gesture made Erik feel good about his employer and about himself because he seemed to quickly regain a feel for his old job. We really appreciated DOD's position and assistance, but after almost a year and a half since the accident, Erik was anxious to return to work. We felt as the therapy people did, that it was time to see if Erik could in fact return and perform his job or not so he could either work or seek training in another area. DOD agreed to put Erik back to work but only part-time to begin with so it would not overtire him. After just two weeks working under this arrangement, Erik was begging to go full-time. He felt he had proven he was able to do the work, and his supervisors agreed. We, of course, were all very grateful that Erik was doing better than anyone (but himself) expected. He was not only relearning the things he knew and did before (including reading schematics) but was also learning new procedures and products as well, all of which further amazed us, his employers, and his therapists. Erik has admitted to experiencing some stress and frustration at work and at being mad at a few less-understanding people from time to time, but for the greater part, he was accepted and treated very well by his coworkers and friends.

As time passed, Erik's circle of single friends dwindled as they got married, bought homes, and had children. Erik became a little fearful that he would never have the opportunity to do any of those things himself. He requested a father's blessing and was reminded by the Lord of the blessing he received in the hospital while in a coma: he was promised that he would be a husband and a father in time. He and we all prayed that he would meet the special person the Lord was preparing for him. Two or three days later, one of Erik's coworkers (JoAnn) showed Erik a picture of her niece and offered to line them up. Erik must have felt that warm, fuzzy feeling and was eager to meet

Sam (Sandra Delaney) as soon as possible even though she lived in the distant town of Grantsville. I don't know what the arrangement was to get Erik and Sam together, but I remember coming home one evening and finding a cute girl in Erik's room alone playing a video game. When I was introduced to Sam, I felt there was something very special about her. Erik and Sam seemed to really enjoy being together, and they dated as frequently as possible. The gloomy Erik we had been seeing transformed to a happy and optimistic person. We felt good about Sam and prayed that she was feeling the same about Erik and the rest of us. She was almost too good to be true but was exactly what we were all praying for. She came from a solid LDS family of seven children, she being the only daughter of Roger and Faye Delaney. I told Erik that he had better treat Sam very well or her six brothers would work him over! The Delaney family treated Erik very well and accepted him "as is" since they never knew him before the accident. It was great to see Erik so happy.

Erik and Sandra were married on June 19, 1998, in Grantsville. They moved into the new home they had built on the day they returned from their honeymoon, and as I mentioned previously, they are the parents of two wonderful sons, Levi and Khristian. We often tried to counsel Erik to be patient and take his time to accomplish his goals, but he must have thought he had better hurry and get things done as soon as possible. Erik and Sam had their marriage sealed and had Levi sealed to them in the Manti Temple in June 1999 (Khristian was "BIC": born in the covenant), so they are indeed an eternal family. All that's left now for Erik is to be a faithful husband and father, obey the Lord, be an example of righteous living, and endure to the end—whenever that will be.

ABOUT THE AUTHOR

My life is end on March 29, 1994. I was reborn in a new life and respect. How precious and quickly change life for multiple people. I finally have time to let people for don't give up easy. But work as hard as you want and think a different way for your success in the new life.

CPSIA information can be obtained
at www.ICGtesting.com
Printed in the USA
BVHW051341301121
622873BV00010B/587